M000031591

# Babies Are Such a Nice Way to Start People

Compiled by Liesl Vazquez

Illustrated by Amy Dietrich

PETER PAUPER PRESS, INC.

WHITE PLAINS, NEW YORK

Design by Arlene Greco

Copyright © 1997
Peter Pauper Press, Inc.
202 Mamaroneck Avenue
White Plains, NY 10601
ISBN 0-88088-824-5
Printed in China
7 6 5 4 3 2 1

# Babies Are Such a Nice Way to Start People

Congratulations! Your new baby will bring many exciting changes to your life, including lots of love, increased responsibilities, and late-night feedings! Enjoy this special time of infancy and savor the sweet moments as you watch for new movements, smiles, and

mastered tasks. And whether
this is your first or your fifth,
remember, as Karen Anderson,
mother of quintuplets, said,
*Children . . . can bring out
the best in you!*

*L. V.*

I was awake for the whole
unbelievable birth. It was so
emotional I sobbed through the
entire experience. . . . And then I saw
the doctor lift him up. It is the single
most amazing experience a human
being could ever have.

*Kathie Lee Gifford*

I was a mother.
I wanted to laugh.
I wanted to cry. I felt
such pride, such an incredible
sense of wholeness.

*Diahann Carroll*

When I first came out from under the anesthesia and opened my eyes to see my baby, my heart filled with love and thanks to God for sending her to me. How can I express how I felt the first time I held her and her blue eyes gazed up into mine? How can you describe a miracle?

*Annette Funicello*

My child looked at me and
I looked back at him in the delivery
room, and I realized that out of
a sea of infinite possibilities it had
come down to this: a specific person,
born on the hottest day of the year,
conceived on a Christmas Eve,
made by his father and me
miraculously from scratch.

*Anna Quindlen*

Childbirth is more
admirable than conquest,
more amazing than self-defense,
and as courageous
as either one.

*Gloria Steinem*

The baby was a lovely little boy,
but sad to say, he did not weigh sixty
pounds. That is what I had gained
and that was what I had to lose.

*Barbara Bush*

This baby is a miracle.
It's like God nodding and saying,
"I'm  pleased with what
you've done."

*Ann Jillian*

For any normal woman in normal
circumstances there is bound to
be a special excitement and joy and
gratitude to God when she
holds her first baby in her arms.

*Rose Fitzgerald Kennedy*

If new-borns could remember
and speak, they would emerge from
the womb carrying tales
as wondrous as Homer's.

*Newsweek*

Is he not beautiful? He's my little
man, my sweetie pie boy, my big guy.
Isn't he delicious? Don't you
want to eat him up?

*Jamie Lee Curtis*

The arrival of Julia was a personal, almost selfish pleasure, the kind that comes when another small person joins the cast of characters and enters the circle of those to care about, wonder about and watch.

*Ellen Goodman*

You fall in love, instantly.
I thought he was the most
beautiful boy I had ever seen.

*Rosie O'Donnell*

The smell of his silky head, the clutch of minuscule fingers against my breast as he nursed. Cleaning him, caring for him, dressing him in soft cottons—doing a good job with my baby brought me free-floating joy.

*Linda Gray Sexton*

It doesn't matter how many
books you read before your baby
arrives; nothing gets you ready for
that first night when you're out of
the hospital and alone, and she's
crying and won't stop, and you're
holding her against you while her
screams rock your chest.

*Bob Greene*

$\bigcirc$nce we had the baby, my wife hit the ground running. She had this innate ability to be a parent from the second of birth. This is not me. I want to be the perfect father, but it doesn't come organically. I'm comfortable holding and touching the baby, but then I forget about him. I'll be like, "Okay, I'm going out now—oh, I can't because I'm watching the baby!"

*Paul Reiser*

I didn't know how I could
possibly love someone [else] as much
as Nayib, and it's a mind-blowing
experience. That's where the song
"Along Came You" comes from,
because love just keeps surprising
you over and over.

*Gloria Estefan*

When a child enters the world
through you, it alters everything on
a psychic, psychological and purely
practical level. You're just not free
anymore to do what you want to do.
And it's not the same again. Ever.

*Jane Fonda*

Babies are unreasonable;
they expect far too much of
existence. Each new generation that
comes takes one look at the world,
thinks wildly, "Is *this* all they've done
to it?" and bursts into tears.

*Clarence Day*

E very baby born into the world is a
finer one than the last.

*Charles Dickens*

We adopted her because she is
meant for us and she is very,
very special.

*Nicole Kidman*

Being a parent is so overwhelming, you could cry just looking at your child. It's an overwhelming feeling of love, of wanting to protect him from any pain, any hurt. And the joy! He makes me laugh. I'm the happiest I've ever been. I feel completely fulfilled.

*Kelly Preston*

If you bungle raising your children,
I don't think whatever else you
do well matters very much.

*Jacqueline Kennedy Onassis*

I looked on child rearing not only
as a work of love and duty but
as a profession that was fully as
interesting and challenging as any
honorable profession in the world
and one that demanded the best
that I could bring to it.

*Rose Fitzgerald Kennedy*

My children have determined my
life; since the day they were born
I have never thought of myself
as an individual but as part of an
inseparable trio.

*Isabel Allende*

I knew having a baby would teach
me about deep feelings of love,
but I didn't know it would teach
me so much about sharing.

*Deidre Hall*

$M$y kids are my
greatest achievements.

*Christie Brinkley*

Of all the roles I've played,
none has been as fulfilling
as being a mother.

*Annette Funicello*

Every [college] commencement should include at least one piece of gratuitous advice, and here is mine: Make babies! Have children — lots of them . . . They are your wager on the future, your gift to society, and the most useful, fulfilling graduate course you will ever take.

*Mitchell E. Daniels, Jr.*

It's just so totally pleasurable
to watch this little guy, to have this
little guy. I don't know what, just to
be with him, to have him love me,
have him need me, to watch him
change and laugh.

*Kate Grimes Weingarten*

If I have to live differently, sell my house, give up certain things in order to do motherhood the right way, then that's what I'm going to do.

*Jamie Lee Curtis*

I needed to achieve a certain
amount of things myself. Once
I felt I achieved a lot of that, then I
started to think I'd like to be able to
pass along knowledge, love, all kinds
of things I've accumulated.

*Donna Mills*

I feel energetic enough to keep
up with [my son]. He has the
power to light up a room.
He positively glows.

*Christie Brinkley*

I'm hard on people.
I tend not to be forgiving of people's
imperfections. But being a mother
has changed me because you can't
be perfect and be a good parent.
Every day is an improvisation.

*Michelle Pfeiffer*

You learn that taking care of yourself is something you do in order to take care of the child. You have to keep yourself alive so that they can rely on you. You have to give them a consistent environment where they can be fed and bathed and clothed and entertained and educated and loved and not necessarily in that order.

*Carrie Fisher*

I still love working, but motherhood definitely comes first. It is the biggest challenge in my life. But it also gave me real security. My greatest accomplishment was giving birth to AJ. He dwarfs the importance of anything else.

*Mary Hart*

$M$y children are my life.
I can't think of anything
that gives me greater joy.

*Jane Seymour*

If I hadn't had a child, I'd never have known that most elemental, direct, true relationship. I don't know if I'd fully understand the values of society that I prize. I would have missed some of the mystery of life and death. Not to know how a child grows, the wonder of a newborn's hand. . . .
I have been fortunate.

*Dianne Feinstein*

While everything else in our lives
has gotten simpler, speedier, more
microwavable and user-friendly,
child-raising seems to have expanded
to fill the time no longer
available for it.

*Barbara Ehrenreich*

We live exactly the way our parents lived. I couldn't imagine hiring a nanny and having a stranger take care of my kids. There's simply no way I'd go out the door without them.

*Bill and Kae Skinner*

There are only two lasting bequests
we can hope to give our children.
One of these is roots;
the other, wings.

*Hodding Carter*

For the first six months of Justin's life, stuff just seemed to ooze from his mouth without warning, and he acquired a widespread reputation for ruining people's shirts.

*Wendy Candliss*

I'm a better writer
because I'm a mother—every day
I see the world through the
eyes of my three children.

*Anna Quindlen*

I have been slow to understand that
the contrariness of the "terrible twos"
is the bloody-mindedness of little
people trying to get a grip on their
partially formed selves. . . .
I no longer think that what
two-year-olds say is nonsense.

*George Will*

Once a year, those of us who
are already mothers should tip our
hats to the truth. Ultimately, children
don't fit into a schedule. They expand
it, complicate it, enrich it. In the
motherhood business, time is
still more crucial than
timing, timing, timing.

*Ellen Goodman*

Mothers soon discover that they are often the only ones who recognize and appreciate all the beauty and complexity of their babies. It comes as a frequent disappointment to us to have our child's range of behaviors and abilities, which seem so marvelous to us, go essentially unnoticed by the rest of the world.

*Deborah Insel*

Spock, shlock, don't talk to me
about that stuff. A man doesn't
know how to bring up children
until he's been a mother.

*Dan Greenburg*

[In a big family] the first child is kind of like the first pancake. If it's not perfect, that's okay, there are a lot more coming along.

*Antonin Scalia*

Before I got married I had
six theories about bringing up
children; now I have six children
and no theories.

*John Wilmot, Earl of Rochester*

When I felt the baby move inside me
for the first time—a tiny tickle,
a butterfly wing brushing my insides—
I was stunned. Now he was no longer
an image in a sonogram, a picture in a
child development book, an idea,
a series of possible names. He defined
himself with that one motion and
made himself heard . . .

*Linda Gray Sexton*

People who claim to have
carefree, regenerative holidays
accompanied by their small children
are either lying or self-deluded.
Family travel has rewards,
but never the ones you expect.

*Marni Jackson*

$P$eople who say they sleep like a
baby usually don't have one.

*Leo J. Burke*

When my kids become wild and
unruly, I use a nice, safe playpen.
When they're finished, I climb out.

*Erma Bombeck*

The art of being a parent is to sleep
when the baby isn't looking.

*Anonymous*

There is this to be said about little children. They keep you feeling old.

*Jean Kerr*

$A$dam and Eve had many
advantages, but the principal one was
that they escaped teething.

*Mark Twain*

Parents of young children should realize that few people, and maybe no one, will find their children as enchanting as they do.

*Barbara Walters*

Babies are competent individuals
who have their own agendas and
should be treated with respect.

*Ruth Mason*

More than in any other human
relationship, overwhelmingly more,
motherhood means being
instantly interruptible,
responsive, responsible.

*Tillie Olsen*

You see your child as a companion
with the qualities you have or
would like to have.

*Naemi Stilman, M.D.*

At every level children are both
creative and the objects of creativity,
for they are literally making
themselves and being made at the
same time. Parents are therefore
constantly being re-made as well.

*Fraser Harrison*

Every mother is like Moses.
She does not enter the promised
land. She prepares a world
she will not see.

*Pope Paul VI*

Ah, baby! little dost thou know
How many yearning bosoms glow,
How many lips in blessings move,
How many eyes beam looks of love
  At sight of thee!

*Joanna Baillie*

Mothers can forgive *anything!*

*Louisa May Alcott,*

Jo's Boys

[S]asha] was everything
I ever wanted. I felt like his soul
was supposed to be with us.

*Pam Light*

What is the little one thinking about?
Very wonderful things, no doubt;
    Unwritten history!
    Unfathomed mystery!
Yet he chuckles, and crows, and nods,
    and winks,
As if his head were as full of kinks
And curious riddles as any sphinx! . . .

*Josiah Gilbert Holland*